GBE

DEVOTIONAL

JUNE 2024:
The Month of
Mind Renewal

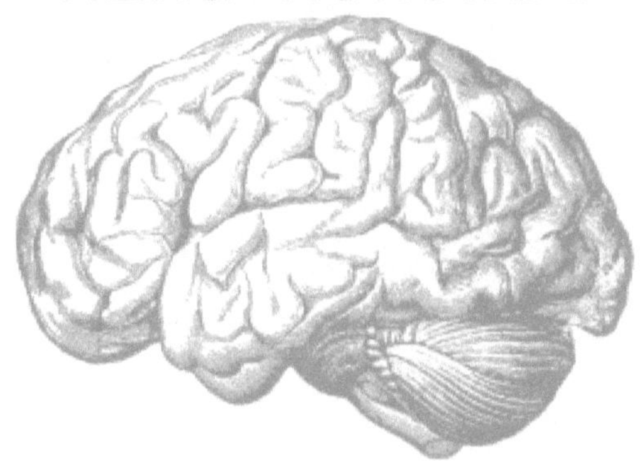

Revealing The Power of
A New Mindset

MUKARO MATUHWA

JUNE:
MONTH OF MIND
RENEWAL
(Rom. 12:2)

A Gift To

....

From

Mukaro Matuhwa

....

JUNE EDITION

Declaration

I **Mukaro Matuhwa** declare that the contents of this book are all mine & none was plagiarized nor copied from anyone or any devotion organization except where I've quoted from the original source (Bible). Many thanks are due to our Lord Jesus Christ for the unmatched wisdom & rare inspiration contained herein. Feel free to allow the Holy Spirit to speak to you on how to level mountains in your endeavors as you will be reading each & every daily devotion. Thank you for being part of the readership. *Signature:*.......................

JUNE EDITION

Copyright

Full or partial reproduction of this copy by any means or form of production is prohibited. Violation of this copyright is a solid crime according to CM Publishers publishing terms & conditions. All rights reserved. Copyright © 2024 CM Publishers.

All rights reserved.

MIND RENEWAL

First Edition: 01 June 2024

Book Cover Design: CMP Designers

Editing & Proof Reading: CMP Editors

Book Cover Art: CMP Designers

Interior Design: CM Publishers

Book Publisher © CMP

JUNE EDITION

Table of Contents

Contents

Declaration

Copyright

Table of Contents

Author's Desk

Theme: Renewal Of The Mind

(Romans 12:2)

Theme: New Creature In Christ

(2 Corinthians 5:17)

Theme: Renewal Of Days

(Lamentations 5:21)

Theme: Knowledge Renewal

(Colossians 3:8-11)

Theme: An Open Shame

(Hebrews 6:4-6)

Theme: Renewal Of Your Bows

(Job 29:15-20)

Theme: A Steadfast Spirit

(Psalm 51:10-13)

Theme: New Wine Overflow

(Proverbs 3:5-10)

Theme: Renewed Strength

(Isaiah 40:28-31)

Theme: Renewed Kingdom

(1 Samuel 11:12-15)

Theme: A New Thing

(Numbers 16:28-32)

Theme: A New Bowl With Salt

(2 Kings 2:19-22)

Theme: The Good News Day

(2 Kings 7:5-9)

Theme: Sing A New Song

(Psalm 40:1-5)

Theme: The Renewal Of Your Youthfulness

(Psalm 103:1-6)

Theme: Nothing New Here

(Ecclesiastes 1:4-9)

Theme: Being Made Into A New Threshing Sledge

(Isaiah 41:13-15)

Theme: Declare New Things

(Isaiah 42:6-9)

Theme: Ordained A Prophet

(Jeremiah 1:5)

Theme: Called By A New Name

(Isaiah 62:1-4)

Theme: Your Descendants

(Isaiah 66:22)

Theme: You are A God

(Psalm 82:1-8)

Theme: New Mercies

(Lamentations 3:22-27)

Theme: A New Spirit

(Ezekiel 11:17-19)

Theme: Hills Flowing Milk

(Joel 3:18)

Theme: New Testament

(Mathew 26:26-28)

Theme: One New Doctrine

(Mark 1:27-28)

Theme: Speak In New Tongues

(Mark 16:17-18)

Theme: Desire New Levels

(Luke 5:35-39)

Theme: Continuous Renewal

(2 Corinthians 4:16)

Salvation Call
Contact Details

JUNE EDITION

Author's Desk

S

eason greetings my dear Reader! I hope to find you well, fit & safe. I found it good if not the best thing to compile these teachings about creativity for you to start to move in paradoxes with a creative approach. So, basing on Romans 12:2 as this month's theme verse, I've written 30 mind renewal teachings that are in a progressive way such that any believer who is eager to live a new lifestyle based on a new mindset in this new year & in this new month of June can easily follow for his or her own beneficiation. Exploits are done as a result of you having a new mindset for you are a god (a spirit man living in a physical body & having a human experience) on earth. A new mindset has the capacity to bring healing (favor, increase & or overflow) to everything that concerns you; be it social life, business life, calling, ministry, finances, physical & or mental health etc. Be ready to embrace a shift in your entire life as you will be going through the pages of this devotional booklet in this month of Mind Renewal.

JUNE EDITION

Theme: Renewal Of The Mind
(Romans 12:2)

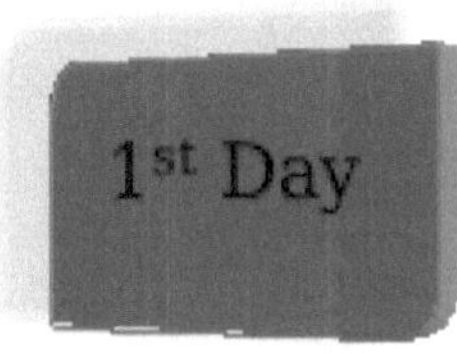

"And be not conformed to this world: but be ye transformed by the renewing of your mind, that ye may prove what is that good and acceptable, and perfect, will of God. For I say, through the grace given unto me, to every man that is among you, not to think of himself more highly than he ought to think; but to think soberly, according as God hath dealt to every man the measure of faith."

NEW CONFESSION:
My mind has been renewed & I'm now thinking of myself & everyone around me soberly! I've a new

W elcome to June – the month of Mind Renewal! In this month, I pray for you that your mind is going to be renewed to the extent that you will never be conformed to this world but you will be transformed (changed totally) by the renewal of your mind. The renewal of the mind has the ability to change your life for as the man thinketh so is he (Proverbs 23:7)! Whatever you are to think of about you becoming in the future in your heart (seeing & feeling in your heart), you'll definitely become it! Today, we are praying for your mind to be renewed such that you start to have a new mindset – a mindset of a king & priest – this is so because it is only those with kingly & priestly mindsets that are going to reign in this world (Revelation 5:10). We have been made kings & priests, so we have to see & honor each other with dignity. You're wise! You're blessed! You're favoured! You are graced! This week is graced! This month is graced!

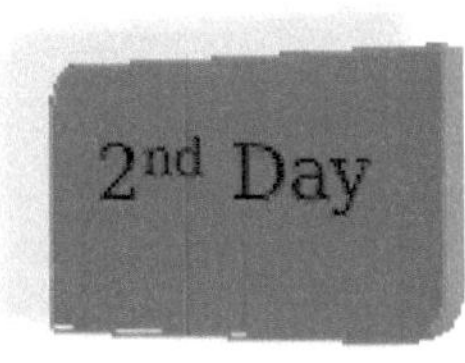

JUNE EDITION

Theme: New Creature In Christ
(2 Corinthians 5:17)

2ⁿᵈ Day

"Therefore, if any man be in Christ, he is a new creature: old things are passed away; behold, all things are become new."

NEW CONFESSION:
I'm in Christ! I'm a new creature in Christ – old things have passed away! New better things are coming now!

W herever you go & in whatever you are to do, always have this new mentality in you that you are in Christ & you are a new creature – a superior being far above & beyond this humanistic realm. You are now a new & rare specie (breed) of beings, thus gods (Psalm 82:6)! Old things (humanistic experience & old knowledge) have passed away, behold all things have become anew now! The supernatural experience & knowledge have come into your life! You will never see shame in your life! You will move from greater glory to greater glory (Proverbs 4:18)! A glorious lifestyle is & shall be your lifetime portion! Your daily provision is going to be supernatural & you shall never lack (Psalm 23:1)! You shall be fruitful & multiplying in & out of season for you've been called into a lifestyle of full dominion, all-round fruitfulness & multiplication

(Genesis 1:28)! You're rich! You're a king! You are a royal member! 1 Peter 2:9 says & I quote, *"But ye are a chosen generation, a royal priesthood, a holy nation, a peculiar people; that ye should shew forth the praises of him who hath called you out of darkness into his marvellous light."*

JUNE EDITION

Theme: Renewal Of Days
(Lamentations 5:21)

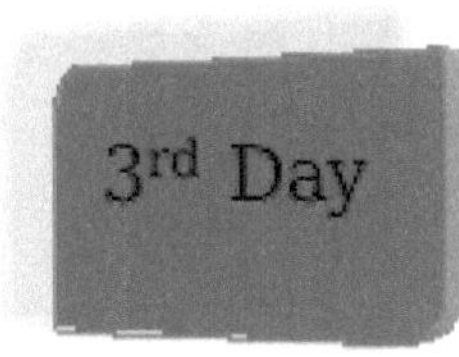

"Turn thou us unto thee, O Lord, and we shall be turned; renew our days as of old."

NEW CONFESSION:
The Lord has turned me; I have a new heart now! My days (life) have been renewed! I'm new! I'm fresh!

Today, allow God to turn you & your heart unto Him till you are turned. What is to be turned by God? What will you be turned into? Turned by God turns you into a god (Psalm 82:6). Turned by God turns you into a supernatural being! Turned by God turns you into a superior being! Turned by God turns you into a king & a priest! Turned by God turns you into a filthily rich man & or woman (Proverbs 10:22)! Turned by God turns you into a well of wisdom! Turned by God turns you into a fountain of life! Turned by God turns you into a new wave of glory & prosperity (Isaiah 43:19)! Turned by God turns you into a realm full of possibilities & immaculate blessings! Turned by God turns you into a city of eternal refuge where no harm shall by any means hurt you (Luke 10:19)! Let this be your prayer today that O Lord turn to me, turn me till I'm turned & then renew my days as of old! In other words, let this be your prayer today that O Lord create in me a new heart (turn me) & renew a steadfast spirit within me (Psalm 51:10)! Your steadfast spirit has to have a continuous renewal for you to excel in all spheres of this life!

JUNE EDITION

Theme: Knowledge Renewal
(Colossians 3:8-11)

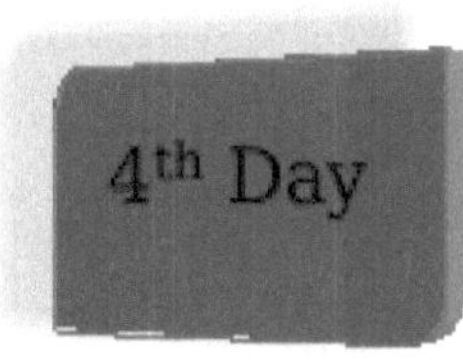

"But now ye also put off all these; anger, wrath, malice, blasphemy, filthy communication out of your mouth. Lie not one to another, seeing that ye have put off the old man with his deeds; & have put on the new man, which is renewed in knowledge after the image of him that created him: where there is neither Greek nor Jew, circumcision nor uncircumcision... bond nor free: but Christ is all, and in all."

A

s new knowledge is coming upon & in you, build in you the capacity to unlearn old things (habits, practises, actions, principles etc.), learn new better things & relearn all good but forgotten things as well. Knowledge is power, they say so, but to me knowledge without application is as simple as death. Applied knowledge is life! Whatever you have learnt, kindly put it into good use (thus, into an application). Take away anger, wrath, malice, blasphemy & all kinds of filthy communication out of your mouth! Learn to speak with & in grace! Put away lies! Abstain from sexual immorality! Put off the old man with his deeds (the way a snake shell off its outer aged skin) & put on the new man which is renewed in knowledge (life) after the image of Him who created him. The new man has no segregation in him – he loves all people the same for he is like Christ (taking form from Christ). Christ is in you & He is the hope of your glory (Col. 1:27).

JUNE EDITION

Theme: An Open Shame
(Hebrews 6:4-6)

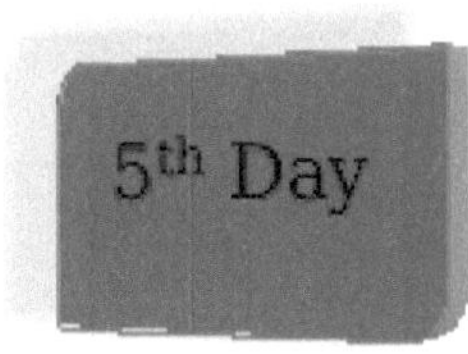

"For it is impossible for those who were once enlightened,
& have tasted of the heavenly gift, and were made partakers of the Holy Ghost, &
have tasted the good word of God, and the powers of the world to come, if they shall
fall away, to renew them again unto repentance; seeing they crucify to themselves the
Son of God
afresh, and put him to an open shame."

A NEW CONFESSION:
Open shame (a permanent fall away) is never my

's you will be moving in this new month of June which have been declared to be the month of Mind Renewal, allow your mind to be programmed in such a way that the new program (software, information, wisdom & or knowledge) is permanently imprinted (understood) in you (your heart) such that you won't leave it & go back. Allow this kind of enlightenment (new knowledge) you have received to be a lifetime one for if you are to fall away from it, it's impossible for you to be renewed again unto repentance. Don't just be amongst those that will be tasters of the heavenly gifts but be a home (warehouse, powerhouse, workshop & fountain) of heavenly gifts. In other words, be partakers of the Holy

Spirit (the manufacturer of all spiritual gifts). Hear the Word of God & do it accordingly such that you won't be only the hearers of the Word but doers also (James 1:22). Doing the Word will give you an opportunity to break away from the humanistic realm into the supernatural realm (future life)!

JUNE EDITION

Theme: Renewal Of Your Bows
(Job 29:15-20)

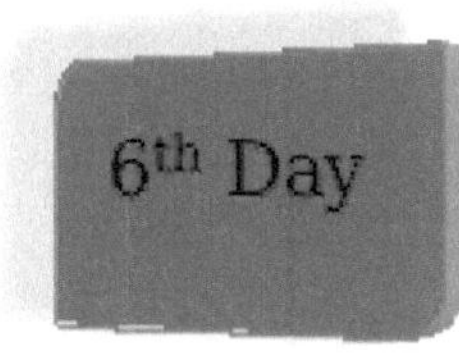

*"I was eyes to the blind & feet was I to the lame.
I was a father to the poor & the cause which I knew not I searched out. And I brake
the jaws of the wicked & plucked the spoil out of his teeth. Then I said, I shall die in
my nest & I shall multiply my days as the sand. My root was spread out by the waters
& the dew lay
all night upon my branch. My glory was fresh in me
and my bow was renewed in my hand."*

D**NEW CONFESSION:**

*My bows (businesses) have been renewed! I'm on a
new & greater horizon now! I speak bigger & better*

o you desire to have fresh glory & to see your own bow (business, company, niche, enterprise etc.) getting renewed in your own hands (tenure of reign)? Here is a tip; be the eyes to the blind – let people see (have knowledge, wisdom & understanding) through you. Be feet to all those that are lame! Let people's lives progress as a result of your eyes (vision) & feet (progress)! Let people get feed from your lips (Proverbs 10:21)! Become a father to the poor (needy) & the blessing of God will surely rest upon you. Be the deliverer of the poor from their (poverty) affliction

(Job 36:15). Give to the poor food (Psalm 22:26) & this is going to break the jaws (chains) of the wicked (poverty). Master your vision, mission & desire to be an expert in your field. Refuse to die in your nest (comfort zone), but rather think big, see big & live big! Spread out all of your businesses & their influence!

JUNE EDITION

Theme: A Steadfast Spirit
(Psalm 51:10-13)

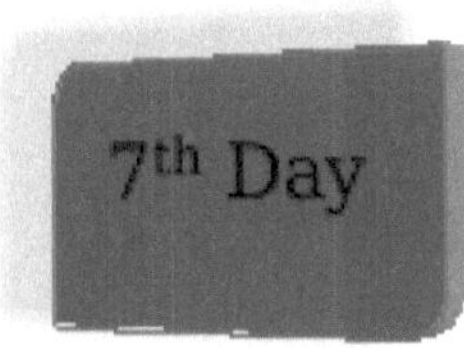

"Create in me a clean heart, O God & renew a right spirit within me. Cast me not away from thy presence; and take not thy holy spirit from me. Restore unto me the joy of thy salvation; and uphold me with thy free spirit. Then will I teach transgressor thy ways; & sinners shall be converted unto thee."

B **NEW CONFESSION:**
I have a new, pure & clean heart now! My spirit has been fully renewed! My joy & love have been restored

efore a right (& or a steadfast) spirit is renewed within you, there is a need of the creation of a new & clean heart in you. You have to have a heart that is a pure & clean! A heart with new & clean thoughts (motives & intentions) for as the man thinks in his heart, so is he (Proverbs 23:7). A pure & clean heart will help you to create a pure, clean, right & favourable environment (atmosphere) for a renewed steadfast spirit to thrive on well (live & conduct its duties in an excellent way). A clean heart is a fountain of life! A clean heart is a stream of joy & love! Pray for God to give you a clean & pure heart such that where ever you go you won't be a burden to people but you will be a blessing. Pray for God not to cast you out & away from His presence, but rather stay & live in His presence till you're filled with His glory & start to shine like what Moses did (Exodus 34:35)! Pray for His Holy Spirit to be outpoured upon you abundantly (Joel 2:28) so that you start to operate well in the realm of unlimited spiritual gifts!

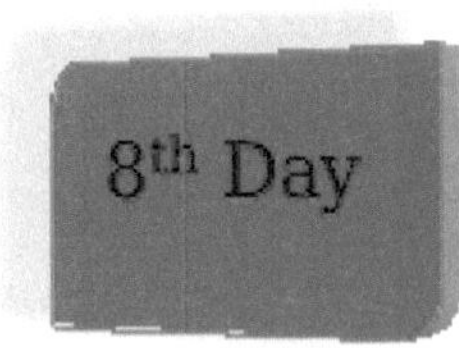

8ᵗʰ Day

"Trust in the Lord with all thine heart; & lean not unto thine own understanding. In all thy ways acknowledge him, & he shall direct thy paths. Be not wise in thine own eyes: fear the Lord & depart from evil. It shall be health to thy navel, & marrow to thy bones. Honour the Lord with thy substance and with the first fruits of all thine increase: so, shall thy barns be filled with plenty, and thy presses shall burst out with new wine."

T

NEW CONFESSION:
I'm going to trust in the Lord day-in, day-out & honor His with my substance so as to live in abundance!

he equation that leads to new wine overflow is simple; trust in the Lord with all your heart + don't lean unto your own understanding (factor in acknowledging God always) = God will direct your paths to the unending sources of new wine. In all your operations, never be wiser than God nor be wise in your own eyes but always submit yourself under God's Word (guidance, counsel, tutorship etc.). Depart from all forms of evil! Flew away from sexual immorality! Resist the devil & he is going to flee away from you & your entire life! Your self-holiness & self-righteousness are going to be health to thy navel & marrow to thy bones! In addition to your self-righteousness, you have to honor the with your substance & with the first fruits of all thine increase – this will lead you into a season where your barns will be filled with plenty & your presses will burst out with new wine!

JUNE EDITION

Theme: Renewed Strength
(Isaiah 40:28-31)

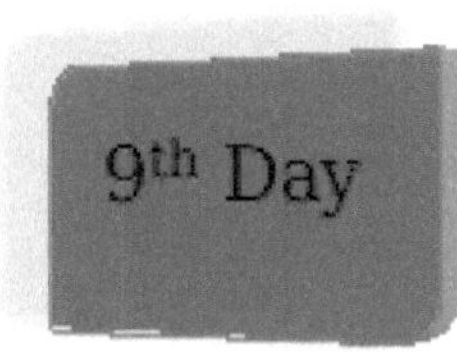

"Hast thou not known? hast thou not heard, that the everlasting God, the Lord, the Creator of the ends of the earth, fainteth not, neither is weary? there is no searching of his understanding. He giveth power to the faint; & to them that have no might he increase strength. Even the youths shall faint and be weary, and the young men shall utterly fall: but they that wait upon the Lord shall renew their strength; they shall mount up with wings as eagles; they shall run, and not be weary; and they shall walk, and not faint."

G

NEW CONFESSION:
Fainting, collapsing, getting weary & failing are never my portion! I'm healthy & strong in & out of season!

od is our Father (Matthew 6:9), so if He is our Father, we have (carry) His DNA in us (thus, being born of God – 1 John 5:4), hence we become gods (Psalm 82:6). If we are gods for sure, then we all carry (have) all attributes, abilities, capabilities & strengths of our Father. Our Father has never fainted nor get weary (tired) since the genesis began. He was strong, He is still & He shall be forever strong for His origin & end, none knows anything about it. Before the beginning, God was there (Genesis 1:1). Many have tried to search His origin but to no avail for the scriptures (Bible) give us an understanding that there is no ending to & of God (Psalm 92:6). If God is like that, we are obliged by the Word to be like Him! You have already been given power & mightiness (Luke 10:19)! You shall never faint nor get weary but like eagles you're going to soar higher & higher (Proverbs 4:18)!

JUNE EDITION

Theme: Renewed Kingdom
(1 Samuel 11:12-15)

"And the people said unto Samuel, who is he that said, shall Saul reign over us? Bring the men, that we may put them to death. And Saul said, there shall not a man be put to death this day: for today the Lord hath wrought salvation in Israel. Then said Samuel to the people, Come, and let us go to Gilgal, & renew the kingdom there. And all the people went to Gilgal; and there they made Saul king before the Lord in Gilgal; & there they sacrificed sacrifices of peace offerings before the Lord; and there Saul and all the men of Israel rejoiced greatly."

N

NEW CONFESSION:
The kingdom of God in me has been renewed now! I'm strong, revived & eager to reign & subdue kingdoms!

one who believes Christ & in Christ shall never die nor put to death for the Lord has already brough salvation to us & now His full kingdom is us (Luke 17:21). Word went on to say that come & let us go to Gilgal (a place of separation) – to do what in Gilgal? Isaiah 1:18-19 says & I quote, *"Come now, and let us reason together, saith the Lord: though your sins be as scarlet, they shall be as white as snow; though they be red like crimson, they shall be as wool. If ye be willing and obedient, ye shall eat the good of the land."* A place of separation is a place of reasoning from real but temporary darkness (thus, ignorance) into real & permanent light (thus, knowledge, wisdom & understanding). After that is done, then the kingdom is ready to be renewed! Great joy is coming your way! All people in your family are going to rejoice greatly!

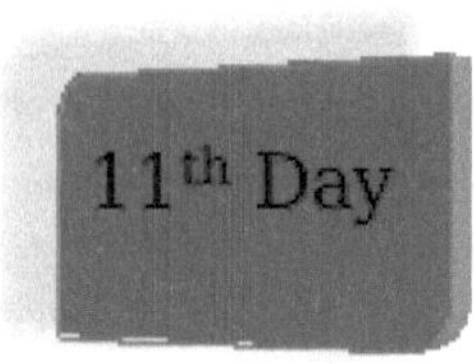

"And Moses said, hereby ye shall know that the Lord hath sent me to do all these works; for I've not done them of my own mind. If these men die the common death of all men, or if they be visited after the visitation of all men; then the Lord hath not sent me. But if the Lord make a new thing & the earth open her mouth & swallow them up, with all that appertain unto them & they go down quick into the pit; then ye shall understand that these men have provoked the Lord. And it came to pass, as he had made an end of speaking all these words, that the ground clave asunder that was under them and the earth opened her mouth & swallowed them up & their houses & all the
men that appertained unto Korah, and all their goods."

T

oday, I have come to challenge all those that for no reason are fighting (& or opposing) you, may the good Lord do something new as a proof that He really called you, anointed you & sent you to do what you are doing. Speak whatever you want to see happening in the camp of your enemies. Moses spoke out an uncommon death (the earth for the first time it opened her mouth & swallowed all that were appertaining unto the camp of Korah) & it became a scripture. Speak what you want to see & God is going to make it a scripture (Living Word) in your life. I prophesy that as you will end speaking those, the manifestation is going to start manifesting in a speedy manner! It is done!

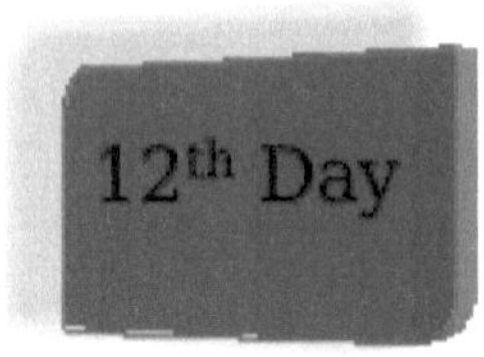

"And the men of the city said unto Elisha, behold, I pray thee, the situation of this city is pleasant, as my lord seeth: but the water is naught & the ground barren. And he said, bring me a new cruse & put salt therein. And they brought it to him. And he went forth unto the spring of the waters, and cast the salt in there & said, thus saith the Lord, I have healed these waters; there shall not be from thence any more death or barren land. So, the waters were healed unto this day, according to the saying of Elisha which he spake."

T

NEW CONFESSION:
My land (nation) has been healed! I'm rising up & shining for the glory of God has risen upon me!

he situation (environment & or atmosphere) of this city (Harare) & nation (Zimbabwe) is pleasant (free, peaceful & safe) but the water (lifestyles economically) is naught & the ground (fields & or markets) are barren (nothing profitable is coming out). Today & not tomorrow, the Prophet of God (Elisha) is saying bring me a new bowl (cruse) with salt therein. Let's go to the springs of the waters (markets) & let's cast the salt in there! Thus saith the Lord, I have healed all these waters (lifestyles), there shall be no more death & or barren businesses! Fruitfulness & multiplication are going to be your daily portion! Business expansion and financial growth shall be your daily norms in & out of season (Isaiah 60:1-5)! Zimbabwe is rising up from the poverty dungeon! This is the season to rise up & shine for His glory is here!

"And they rose up in the twilight, to go unto the camp of the Syrians and when they were come to the uttermost part of the camp of Syria, behold, there was no man there. For the Lord had made the host of the Syrians to hear a noise of chariots and a noise of horses, even the noise of a great host & they said one to another, lo, the king of Israel has hired against us the kings of the Hittites...kings of the Egyptians, to come upon us. Wherefore they arose and fled in the twilight & left their tents & their horses & their asses, even the camp as it was & fled for their life. And when these lepers came to the uttermost part of the camp, they went into one tent & did eat & drink, and carried thence silver & gold & raiment & went & hid it & came again & entered into another tent & carried thence also & went and hid it. Then they said one to another, we do not well: this day is a day of good tidings & we hold our peace: if we tarry till the morning light, some mischief will come upon us...come, that we may go & tell the king's household."

I

NEW CONFESSION:
*I'm the right candidate of good news all year around!
I'm blessed going in & going out! My family is blessed!*

declare & I decree that today is the **GOOD NEWS DAY** to you & your family! Confusion & noise is happening right now in the camp of all of your enemies for God is moving elements on your behalf! Get into your house, car, office, tuckshop, room, yard, mine, stand etc. start to eat, drink & start to make money! Silver & gold are all His (Haggai 2:8)! Peace is coming upon your household! Good news is your daily portion! It shall be good news upon good news, amen!

JUNE EDITION

Theme: Sing A New Song
(Psalm 40:1-5)

"I waited patiently for the Lord & he inclined unto me & heard my cry. He brought me up also out of a horrible pit, out of the miry clay & set my feet upon a rock & established my goings. And he hath put a new song in my mouth, even praise unto our God: many shall see it & fear and shall trust in the Lord. Blessed is that man that maketh the Lord his trust and respect not the proud, nor such as turn aside to lies. Many, O Lord my God, are thy wonderful works which thou hast done & thy thoughts which are towards us: they cannot be reckoned up in order unto thee: if I would declare & speak of them, they are more than can be numbered."

NEW CONFESSION:
I've a new song in my mouth – a song of love, peace, joy grace & prosperity! I shall never lack nor struggle!

If you are to diligently & patiently wait upon the Lord, He shall surely hear you & your cry. Even though you might have been in a horrible pit with miry clay, the Lord is setting you free today! You're coming out of miry clay (poverty, ancestral cages, curses, limitations, delays etc.) today! Your feet are being set upon a rock (Jesus Christ – the owner of cattle on a thousand hills (Psalm 50:10) & the owner of all silver & gold both in heaven & on earth (Haggai 2:8)). The Lord Jesus Christ is the one that is going to establish & map all your on-goings from now onwards! You shall never lack nor struggle for the Lord is putting a new song in your mouth! You're blessed for you've put your trust in God! Great & might works shall you do without any hesitation!

JUNE EDITION

Theme: The Renewal
Of Your Youthfulness
(Psalm 103:1-6)

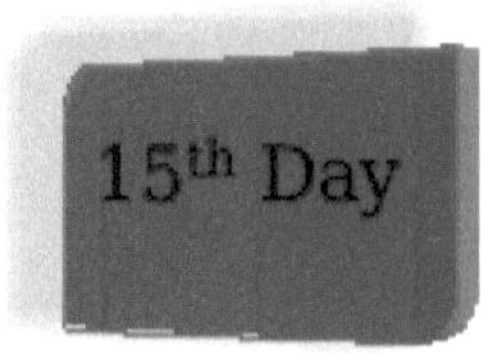

"Bless the Lord, O my soul & all that is within me,
bless His holy name. Bless the Lord, O my soul & forget not
all His benefits: who forgive all thine iniquities; who health all thy diseases; who
redeemeth thy life from destruction; who crowneth thee with lovingkindness and
tender mercies; who satisfieth thy mouth
with good things; so that thy youth is renewed like the eagle's.
The Lord executeth righteousness and judgment
for all that are oppressed."

B

NEW CONFESSION:
My youthfulness has been renewed! I'm forever young,
fresh & upmarket! Excellence is my portion!

efore your youthfulness is renewed like the eagles by God, there has to be some good play (work to be done) in the background. You have to (thus you at a personal level) bless the Lord with your soul (thus, your body & spirit combined – Genesis 2:7). After blessing the Lord, you don't have to wait (& or stop) there, you have to put to remembrance all the benefits of God. The Lord executes righteousness & pure judgement for & on all that are oppressed. Healing is has come upon you, if you have been sick! Your sins have been forgiven, if you have been a sin master! Your life has been fully redeemed – you are no longer imprisoned in sin! The Lord is crowning you with lovingkindness & tender mercies! Glad tidings are your portion! You shall never grow old! No more stress! Your youthfulness is being renewed like now!

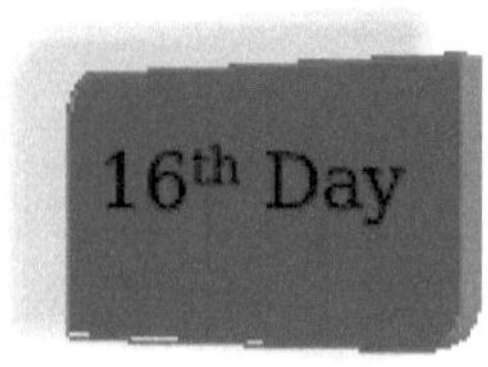

*"One generation passes away & another generation cometh:
but the earth abides for ever. The sun also arises & the sun goes
down & hastes to his place where he arose. The wind goes toward
the south & turns about unto the north; it whirls about continually
& the wind returns again according to his circuits. All the rivers run into the sea; yet
the sea is not full; unto the place from whence the rivers come, thither they return
again. All things are full of labour; man cannot utter it: the eye is not satisfied with
seeing, nor the
ear filled with hearing. The thing that hath been, it is that
which shall be & that which is done is that which shall be
done & there is no new thing under the sun."*

T

NEW CONFESSION:
*I'm going to be stylish & unique in all my dealings so
as to break forth into greatness operating realm!*

he
only thing that is bound to pass away is a generation & not the earth for
the Word says that the earth abides for ever. As time flies away, all things
remain in their post of duty. Nothing shall ever get weary, full nor
tiresome for the Lord renews their strengths on a daily basis. Never ever
get weary of doing good for doing good is like a river running into the

sea. The sea will never get full so is a man unto which good is done to. Keep on doing it! Repeat it till it becomes your lifestyle. There is nothing new under the sun, repeat what was done before but in a different (and stylish) way with a unique approach & let's see if things are not going to turn-around for your good. Change is inevitable! God bless you.

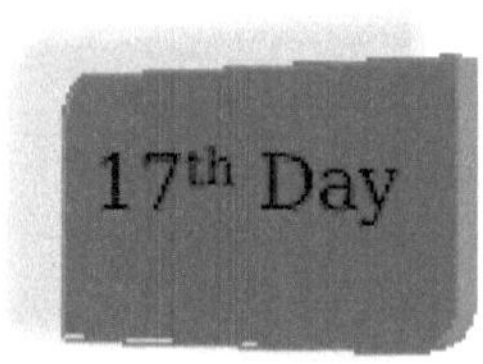

*"For I the Lord thy God will hold thy right hand, saying
unto thee, Fear not; I'll help thee. Fear not, thou worm Jacob,
& ye men of Israel; I'll help thee, saith the Lord, and thy redeemer,
the Holy One of Israel. Behold, I'll make thee a new sharp threshing instrument
having teeth: thou shalt thresh the mountains and
beat them small, & shalt make the hills as chaff."*

F

NEW CONFESSION:
*The Lord has made me a threshing instrument! I'm
bright! I'm untouchable! I'm unstoppable!*

ear nothing in this life nor that to come for the Lord has good plans for you. Jeremiah 29:11-13 says & I quote, ***"For I know the thoughts that I think toward you, saith the Lord, thoughts of peace & not of evil, to give you an expected end. Then shall ye call upon me & ye shall go & pray unto me and I will hearken unto you. And ye shall seek me & find me, when ye shall search for me with all your heart."*** He is going to be with you in & out of season wherever you are to go! Joshua 1:7 says & I quote, ***"There shall not any man be able to stand before thee all the days of thy life: as I was with Moses, so I'll be with thee: I'll not fail thee, nor*** *forsake thee."* None shall be able to stand before you & prevail against you (Joshua of your family) for the Lord is going to make you a new sharp threshing instrument! You shall thresh both small & big mountains (situations, problems & or conspiracies)! Above only shall be your daily testimony (Deuteronomy 28:13)!

JUNE EDITION

Theme: Declare New Things
(Isaiah 42:6-9)

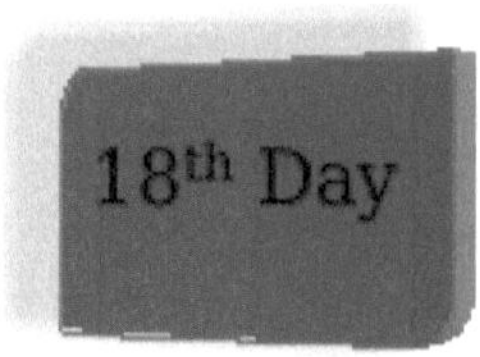

*"I the Lord have called thee in righteousness & will hold
thine hand, & will keep thee & give thee for a covenant of the people, for a light of
the Gentiles; to open the blind eyes, to bring out the prisoners from the prison &
them that sit in darkness out of the prison house. I am the Lord: that is my name: &
my glory will I not give to another, neither my praise to graven images. Behold, the
former things are come to pass, and new things do I declare:
before they spring forth I tell you of them."*

NEW CONFESSION:
*New, great & mighty things are coming my way! I'm
shining & shall continue to shine till eternity!*

D o
you know that each & every believer has a calling from God? For you to
become a believer, you had to first answer God's call that was upon your
life. You had to open the door for Christ to enter. Revelation 3:20 says &
I quote, ***"Behold, I stand at the door & knock: if any man hear my voice
and open the door, I'll come in to him & will sup with him & he with
me."*** The Lord has called you into His righteousness – He is going to
hold thine hand, keep thee & give thee for a covenant & light of the
Gentiles. Matthew 5:14-16 says & I quote, ***"Ye're the light of the world.
A city that is set on a hill cannot be hid. Neither do men light a candle***

& put it under a bushel... Let your light so shine before men, that they may see your good works & glorify your Father which is in heaven." Through your light, the blind shall see & prisoners shall be made free! Wherever you're to go; liberty, progress & prosperity shall follow you!

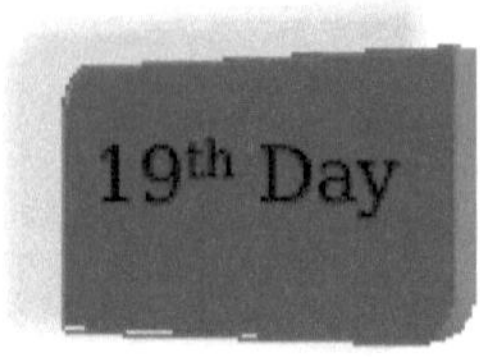

"Before I formed thee in the belly I knew thee; & before thou camest forth out of the womb I sanctified thee & I ordained thee a prophet unto the nations. Then said I, ah, Lord God! behold, I cannot speak: for I'm a child. But the Lord said unto me, say not, I'm a child: for thou shalt go to all that I shall send thee and whatsoever I command thee thou shalt speak. Be not afraid of their faces: for I am with thee to deliver thee, saith the Lord. Then the Lord put forth his hand, & touched my mouth. And the Lord said unto me, Behold, I have put my words in thy mouth. See, I've this day set thee over the nations and over the kingdoms, to root out, and to pull down, and to

destroy, and to throw down, to build, and to plant."

Y es, that prophecy was for Jeremiah but you are free to personalize it today & start to live in its full reality. The Word of God today is saying that before you were formed in the belly of thy mom, the Lord knew thee, sanctified thee & ordained thee a Prophet both to your family & nations around the world. Stand in the gap for the Lord is going to give thee an utterance. Be on the full charge to root out all evil altars, pull down strongholds, destroy evil powers & evil kingdoms, throw down evil thrones, build new kingdoms & plant new things in your life. Fear not! Never be afraid of your enemies, for the Lord is with thee & He is going to help thee! Just be confident in Him for He is able! God bless you.

*"For Zion's sake will I not hold my peace & for Jerusalem's sake
I'll not rest, until the righteousness thereof go forth as brightness & the salvation
thereof as a lamp that burneth. And the Gentiles shall see thy righteousness & all
kings thy glory: & thou shalt be called by a new name, which the mouth of the Lord
shall name. Thou shalt also be a crown of glory in the hand of the Lord & a royal
diadem
in the hand of thy God. Thou shalt no more be termed Forsaken; neither shall thy
land any more be termed Desolate: but thou
shalt be called Hephzibah & thy land Beulah: for the Lord
delighteth in thee & thy land shall be married."*

F

or
your sake, the Lord is saying that He is never going to hold His peace till
your righteousness starts to shine brighter & brighter unto a perfect day
(Proverbs 4:18)! The Lord is never going to rest till your salvation starts
to burn like a lamp & or fire! All Gentiles shall see your righteousness &
all kings shall see your glory! This shall then cause you to be called by a
new name for royalty always recognises royalty! The crown of glory shall

be upon you head for you are a royal diadem in the hand of God. You shall neither be called *Forsaken* nor *Desolate*, for thus shall be called *Hephzibah* which means The Lord's delight. The Lord is about to take delight in you! Be prepared, ready & expectant for you are about to arise & shine for thy light has come (Isaiah 60:1-5).

JUNE EDITION

Theme: Your Descendants
(Isaiah 66:22)

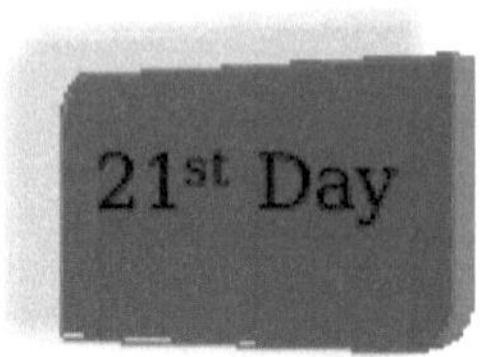

*"For as the new heavens and the new earth,
which I'll make, shall remain before me, saith the Lord,
so shall your seed & your name remain."*

T
NEW CONFESSION:
Myself & my seed (descendants) shall never die but we shall outnumber generations! Long life is my portion!

he Word of God is saying that your seed (descendants) and your name shall remain before the Lord so long the new earth & the new heaven remains before the Lord. In other words, the opening scripture is indirectly saying that you & your seed (descendants) shall outnumber generations for with long life the Lord is going to satisfy you (Psalm 91:16). You shall never die! Psalm 118:17 says & I quote, *"I shall not die, but live & declare the works of the Lord."* Glad tidings are your daily portion! Fruitfulness & multiplication are your lifetime blessings! You shall never struggle to have babies, start & run profitable businesses! From glory to glory shall be your daily confession (Proverbs 4:18)! Your seeds (descendants) are blessed going in & going out! They shall never be tails but they shall all be heads in their all their day-to-day operations; be it in business, social circles, religious circles, financial markets etc. Supernatural intelligence shall be their daily testimony! What your forefathers failed to accomplish over the pass decades & generations, you shall have it in one year! This is that year, start to pursue it now!

JUNE EDITION

Theme: You are A God
(Psalm 82:1-8)

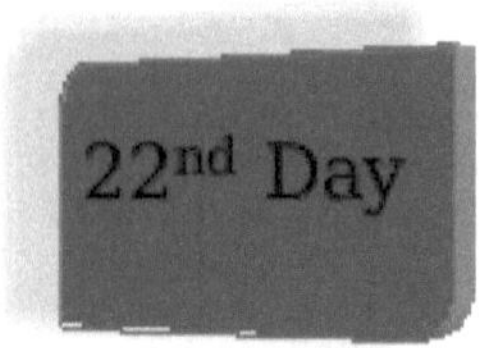

"God standeth in the congregation of the mighty; He judgeth among the gods. How long will ye judge unjustly & accept the persons of the wicked? Selah. Defend the poor & fatherless: do justice to the afflicted & needy. Deliver the poor and needy: rid them out of the hand of the wicked. They know not, neither will they understand; they walk on in darkness: all the foundations of the earth are out of course. I have said, ye are gods & all of you are children of the Most High. But ye shall die like men, and fall like one of the princes. Arise, O God, judge the earth: for thou shalt inherit all nations."

L

NEW CONFESSION:
I'm a god! I'm born of God to overcome the world! I'm going to judge & inherit all nations! I'm a king!

et this new mentality be in you that you are a god (God) for you are a child of God – born of God to overcome the world (1 John 5:4). You have to arise & shine for it is in your shining phase that you are going to judge the earth so as to inherit (rule) all nations! Isaiah 60:1-5 says & I quote, *"Arise, shine; for thy light is come & the glory of the Lord is risen upon thee. For, behold, the darkness shall cover the earth, and gross darkness the people: but the Lord shall arise upon thee, and his glory shall be seen upon thee. And the Gentiles shall come to thy light, and kings to the brightness of thy rising. Lift up thine eyes round about, and see: all they gather themselves together, they come to thee: thy sons shall come from far & thy daughters shall be nursed at thy side."* This is your time & season to shine!

JUNE EDITION

Theme: New Mercies
(Lamentations 3:22-27)

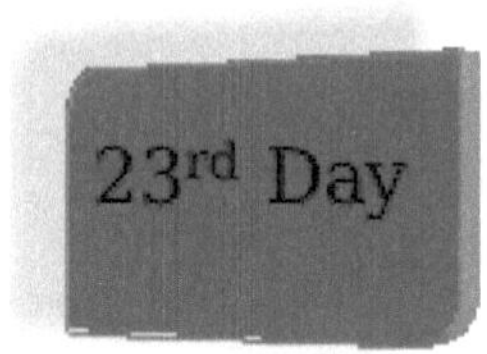

"It is of the Lord's mercies that we are not consumed, because His compassions fail not. They are new every morning: great is thy faithfulness. The Lord is my portion, saith my soul; therefore, will I hope in him. The Lord is good unto them that wait for him, to the soul that seeketh him. It is good that a man should both hope & quietly wait for the salvation of the Lord. It is good for a man that he bear the yoke in his youth."

Y

NEW CONFESSION:
The Lord's mercies are ever new every morning! My floors shall be full & my vats shall overflow!

ou have to be grateful unto God always for it is Him (the Lord) & His mercies that you're not yet consumed. So many violent storms, tornados, floods, veld fires & whirlwinds fiercely came towards & against you, but the Lord put a hedge around you. Job 1:10 says & I quote, ***"Have you not put a hedge around him & his household and everything he has? You have blessed the work of his hands, so that his flocks & herds are spread throughout the land."*** There is a hedge around you! Be glad & rejoice in the Lord! Joel 2:22-24 says & I quote, ***"Be not afraid, ye beasts of the field: for the pastures of the wilderness do spring, for the tree bear*** *her fruit, the fig tree and the vine do yield their strength. Be glad then, ye children of Zion & rejoice in the Lord your God: for he hath given you the former rain moderately & he'll cause to come down for you the rain, the former rain & the latter rain in the first month. And the floors shall be full of wheat & the vats shall overflow with wine & oil."*

JUNE EDITION

Theme: A New Spirit
(Ezekiel 11:17-19)

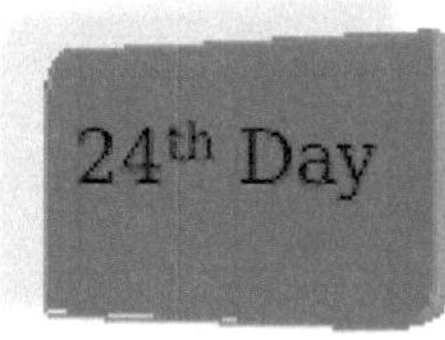

"Therefore say, thus saith the Lord God; I'll even gather you from the people, and assemble you out of the countries where ye have been scattered, and I will give you the land of Israel. And they shall come thither & they shall take away all the detestable things thereof & all the abominations thereof from thence. And I'll give them one heart,
& I will put a new spirit within you & I'll take the stony heart out of their flesh, and will give them a heart of flesh."

W

NEW CONFESSION:
The Spirit of the Lord is upon me! I've a new spirit in me! I've been anointed to preach good news to the

hatever you have lost before, the Lord God of Israel shall gather your lost treasure back, assemble you & restore back all that which you have lost. All abominations & detestable things shall be taken away from you! The Lord shall give you a new heart & a new spirit within you. The stony heart shall be taken out of your flesh by the Lord! A new heart & a new steadfast spirit are coming! You shall be testifying sooner than expected that the Spirit of the Lord (new spirit) will now be upon you! Luke 4:18-19 says & I quote, ***"The Spirit of the Lord is upon me...He hath anointed me to preach the gospel to the poor; he hath sent me to heal the broken-hearted, to preach deliverance to the captives & recovering of sight to the blind, to set at liberty...that are bruised, to preach the acceptable year of the Lord."*** Joel 2:28 says & I quote, ***"...I will pour out my spirit upon all flesh & your sons & your daughters shall prophesy...your young men shall see visions."***

JUNE EDITION

Theme: Hills Flowing Milk
(Joel 3:18)

25th Day

"And it shall come to pass in that day, that the mountains shall drop down new wine, and the hills shall flow with milk, and all the rivers of Judah shall flow with waters, and a fountain shall come forth out of the house of the Lord, and shall water the valley of Shittim."

NEW CONFESSION:
Situations dropping down new wine & milk are my portion! I'm rich! I'm wealthy! I'm blessed!

M ountains in the Bible represent different situations in life. Today, the Word of God (on Joel 3:18) is saying that the mountains (situations) shall drop down new wine (thus, an earthly prosperity – tokens of the blessing of God). Hills shall flow with milk and rivers shall continue flow with waters. Isaiah 43:18-19 says & I quote, ***"Remember ye not the former things, neither consider the things of old. Behold, I'll do a new thing; now it shall spring forth; shall ye not know it? I'll even make a way in the wilderness & rivers in the desert."*** New wine is coming! A new wave of glory & a new dimension of prosperity is coming! Where you have formerly experienced drought (barrenness, losses, rejection etc.), a bumper harvest (fruitful experience) is coming! Good news is coming your way! Where they have plotted an evil report, a good report shall be released! There is no enchantment against you, for you are an elect! You are a small god! Your life is righteous! Proverbs 4:18 says & I quote, *"...the path of the just is as the shining light, that shineth more & more unto the perfect day."*

JUNE EDITION

Theme: New Testament
(Mathew 26:26-28)

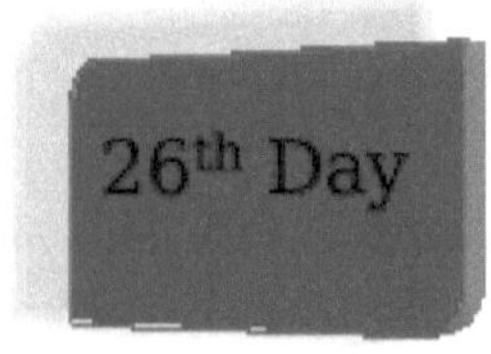

"And as they were eating, Jesus took bread & blessed it & brake it & gave it to the disciples & said, take, eat; this is my body. And he took the cup & gave thanks & gave it to them, saying, drink ye all of it; for this is my blood of the new testament, which is shed for many for the remission of sins."

W

NEW CONFESSION:
I'm in Christ Jesus, therefore I'm a new creature now! All things have passed away! Eternal life is my portion!

e are in the post the New Testament era & we are by far much better than all those that witnessed the end of the New Testament for it was after the death of the testator that eternal life was introduced to us when the graves were opened, the dead people got back to life (resurrected) & death was rendered powerless. 1 Corinthians 15:55-57 says & I quote,

"O death, where is thy sting? O grave, where is thy victory? The sting of death is sin & the strength of sin is the law. But thanks be to God, which giveth us the victory through our Lord Jesus Christ." The New Testament came with Christ's full life (through the bread – thus, His flesh & the wine – thus, His blood). In us, there is no more any mortal DNA nor any trace of death, for we are now in Christ with Christ life! 2 Corinthians 5:17 says & I quote, *"Therefore if any man be in Christ, he is a new creature: old things are passed away; behold, all things are become new."* We are new creatures in Christ that are far above this natural & humanistic realm!

JUNE EDITION

Theme: One New Doctrine
(Mark 1:27-28)

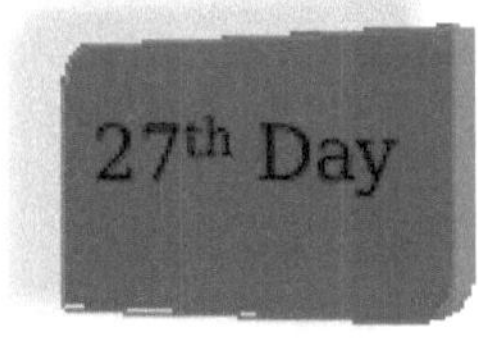

"And they were all amazed, insomuch that they questioned among themselves, saying, what thing is this? What new doctrine is this? For with authority commandeth he even the unclean spirits, & they do obey him. And immediately his fame spread abroad throughout all the region round about Galilee."

O

NEW CONFESSION:
I have power & authority far above my level &

ne new doctrine you have to master is this that you don't have to fear the devil & all of his demons (unclean & or evil spirits) for the Lord has fearfully & wonderfully made you (Psalm 139:14) to be higher than angels (ministering spirits). Hebrews 1:13-14 says & I quote, *"But to which of the angels said he at any time, sit on my right hand, until I make thine enemies thy footstool? Are they not all ministering spirits, sent forth to minister for them who shall be heirs of salvation?"* Psalm 8:4-6 says & I quote, *"What is man, that thou art mindful of him? & the son of man, that thou visits him? For thou hast made him a little lower than the angels & hast crowned him with glory and honour. Thou made him to have dominion over the works of thy hands; thou hast put all things under his feet."* God has crowned you with glory & honor! All things have been put under your feet! Demons are under your feet! Poverty & lack are under your feet! Sickness & diseases are all under your feet! All this is being so just because the Lord has made you to be seated with Christ in heavenly places.

JUNE EDITION

Theme: Speak In New Tongues
(Mark 16:17-18)

"And these signs shall follow them that believe; In my name shall they cast out devils; they shall speak with new tongues; they shall take up serpents & if they drink any deadly thing, it shall not hurt them; they shall lay hands on the sick, and they shall recover."

S

peaking with new tongues is part of the number of the signs that will effortlessly follow them that believe (believers), so you can actually see that it's not only for Pastors nor Prophets nor Evangelists nor Teachers nor Bishops but it's for each & every believer. You don't have to struggle for you to start to speak with new tongues, but you only have to simply believe in God & then God will then give you an utterance through His Holy Spirit. It is the Holy Spirit in you that will move you & push you to have an utterance & never you nor your effort! You don't have to plan nor construct nor put words in order but the Holy Spirit in you will do it for you. Acts 2:4 says & I quote, ***"And they were all filled with the Holy Ghost & began to speak with other tongues, as the Spirit gave them utterance."*** Speak with new tongues with eloquence more than anyone you know can speak with them (1 Cor. 14:18). Don't forbid anyone to speak with new tongues (1 Cor. 14:39). I pray for you now, may the Holy Spirit come upon you now & may you begin to speak with new tongues & prophesy (Acts 19:6)! Receive Him now!

JUNE EDITION

Theme: Desire New Levels
(Luke 5:35-39)

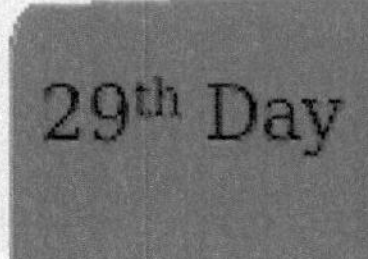

"And he spoke also a parable unto them; no man put a piece of a new garment upon an old; if otherwise, then both the new maketh a rent & the piece that was taken out of the new agree not with the old. And no man put new wine into old bottles; else the new wine will burst the bottles & be spilled & the bottles shall perish. But new wine must be put into new bottles & both are preserved. No man also having drunk old wine straightway desireth new: for he saith, the old is better."

T

> NEW CONFESSION:
> *It's a new level manifesting! It's a new dimension unfolding! I'm prosperous, rich & wealthy!*

he renewed mind, new steadfast spirit & a new clean heart have to be in a new man (new body & or new house) for you can't put new wine (earthly prosperity, wisdom, knowledge, understanding & grace) in an old wineskin (bottle, jar & or mug). For your renewed mind & new steadfast spirit to thrive safely, you have to have a new mindset, new thoughts & new ideas. For your clean heart to remain clean, you have to watch out on your words, actions & habits. You have to diligently keep (safeguard) your heart for out of it follows issues of life (Proverbs 4:23). Desire new grace! Desire new habits! Desire a new mindset – a new way of thinking! Desire new dimensions of prosperity! For it is out of that new level (& or dimension) that your burdens are going to be uplifted, progress mapped & destinies shifted! Embrace a new wave of glory & prosperity that is coming your life now (Isaiah 43:19)! You never struggle nor lack (Psalm 23:1-6).

JUNE EDITION

Theme: Continuous Renewal
(2 Corinthians 4:16)

"We having the same spirit of faith, according as it is written, I believed & therefore have I spoken; we also believe & therefore speak; knowing that he which raised up the Lord Jesus shall raise up us also by Jesus and shall present us with you. For all things are for your sakes, that the abundant grace might through the thanksgiving of many redound to the glory of God. For which cause we faint not; but though our outward man perish, yet the inward man is renewed day by day. For our light affliction, which is but for a moment, work for us a far more exceeding & eternal weight of glory; while we look not at the things which are seen, but at the things which are not seen: for the things which are seen are temporal; but the things which are not seen are eternal."

A
NEW CONFESSION:
Continuous renewal is my portion! I shall be moving from glory to greater glory! No more stagnation!

s we close the curtain of June – which has been a month of Mind Renewal – I want you to continuously have this mindset in you that all things are for your sake. Not some, but all things! Romans 8:25-28 says & I quote, *"But if we hope for that we see not, then do we with patience wait for it. Likewise, the Spirit also helpeth our infirmities: for we know not what we should pray for as we ought: but the Spirit itself maketh intercession for us with groanings which cannot be uttered. And he that searcheth the hearts knoweth what is the mind of the Spirit, because he maketh intercession for the saints according to the will of God. And we know that all things work together for good to them that love God, to them who are the called according to his purpose."* All things will work out for your good for you know that all afflictions are temporary & they come with a mandate to work for your far more exceeding & eternal weight of glory. All things work for good for you because you know that at all levels (both stressing & jovial) the Spirit helps our infirmities, for at times you don't what you should pray for as you ought but the Spirit makes intercession for you with groanings (thus, having travailings in the spirit) which cannot be uttered. Though the outwards appearance seems to be deeming or perishing, the inner man is getting renewed day-in, day-out. A greater glory is coming – the glory that is far beyond your imaginations! You have seen it correctly that I have written that a greater glory is coming your way, yes, it's true; believe it, speak it & then be ready & expectant to see it coming into manifestation (thus, having it in reality). Continuous renewal is your portion! You shall never lack nor struggle for the Lord shall be your supernatural providence! It is done! God bless you, shalom.

MARCH EDITION

Salvation Call

Scripture: Romans 10:13 "For whoever calls on the name of the Lord shall be saved".

Prayer: Thank you, Lord, Jesus Christ for your Word which says that whosoever believes in your word & calls upon your name shall be saved. I therefore, come to you today confessing that I'm a sinner. May you forgive me all my sins. I believe in you, O Lord Jesus Christ that you died for my sins on the cross & on the third day you rose up from the dead full of power, life, grace & glory. O Lord, Jesus Christ, come into my heart, be my Lord & my Saviour. Lead me & guide me in all my errands from today onwards. I'm now yours, take control of me. Thank you, O Lord for saving my soul. I've eternal life now in the name of Jesus Christ, amen.

MARCH EDITION

Contact Details

Charity Monday Publishers
t/a CM Publishers
4009 Ebenezer, Southgate, Harare South
Mobile: +263774571035/
+263737183626
www.facebook.com/cmpublishers[1]
Linkedin Account: Mukaro Matuhwa
Facebook Account: Mkaro Mathwa
Email: tmmatuhwa@gmail.com
Instagram: @mmathwa

---

1. http://www.facebook.com/cmpublishers

his

T is a devotional booklet that was written by Mukaro Matuhwa who was born & bred in Masvingo. Mukaro Matuhwa did his elementary primary education at Mbuyanehanda Primary School, his secondary education at Silveira High School & his tertiary education at Harare Institute of Technology. He is eyeing to be a unique devotional author, acme engineer & a seasoned Message believer. March: Month of Mind Renewal is a Romans 12:2 based devotional booklet that I've written with mind renewal teachings that are in a progressive way such that any believer who is eager to live a new lifestyle based on a new mindset in this new year & in this new month of June can easily follow for his or her own beneficiation. Exploits are done as a result of you having a new mindset for you are a god (a spirit man living in a physical body & having a human experience) on earth. A new mindset has the capacity to bring healing (favor, increase & or overflow) to everything that concerns you; be it social life, business life, calling, ministry, finances, physical & or mental health etc. Be ready to embrace a shift in your entire life as you will be going through the pages of this devotional booklet in this month of Mind Renewal.